CEO Guide to Doing Business in China

By Ade Asefeso MCIPS MBA

Second Edition

ISBN-13: 978-1499543209

ISBN-10: 1499543204

Publisher: AA Global Sourcing Ltd
Website: http://www.aaglobalsourcing.com

Table of Contents

Disclaimer

This publication is designed to provide competent and reliable information regarding the subject matter covered. However, it is sold with the understanding that the author and publisher are not engaged in rendering professional advice. The authors and publishers specifically disclaim any liability that is incurred from the use or application of contents of this book.

Dedication

This book is dedicated to the hundreds of thousands of incredible souls in the world who have weathered through the up and down of recent recession.

To my family and friends who seems to have been sent here to teach me something about who I am supposed to be. They have nurtured me, challenged me, and even opposed me.... But at every juncture has taught me!

This book is dedicated to my lovely boys, Thomas, Michael and Karl. Teaching them to manage their finance will give them the lives they deserve. They have taught me more about life, presence, and energy management than anything I have done in my life.

Chapter 1: Why China?

China is the great economic success story of the past 30 years. Since the "reform and opening-up" policy was introduced in 1978, China has changed beyond recognition. A Soviet-styled planned economy has transformed into a vibrant market-oriented economy and 400 million people have been lifted out of poverty.

Well known for its manufacturing capability, China is the largest global producer of toys, textiles, washing machines, cameras and computers (among hundreds of other products).

It is also the world's largest consumer of iron, steel, coal and cement, and China's hunger for raw materials continues. Over a million enterprises have flourished, and over 40 Chinese companies have entered the global Fortune 500 list.

With rapid and continuous industrialisation and urbanisation, a vast and fast-growing consumer market has emerged. Bicycles and Mao suits have been substituted by over 14 million cars (now the largest car market in the world), international labels and luxury goods. China is also the world's largest ICT market, with over 600 million mobile users and more than 400 million internet users. Private consumerism continues to develop with greater sophistication.

Driving Global Economic Recovery

While many of the world's major economies are still struggling to recover from economic contraction, China's growth has been sustained and the economy grew 8.7 per cent in 2009, the best performance of all major economies.

There are significant changes in China's growth strategy. Traditionally, China has provided low-cost manufacturing solutions for the global market, but exports declined sharply after the global downturn and China's manufacturing industry has responded by quickly moving up the value chain.

The Government is pressing hard to improve infrastructure and social welfare as well as targeting resources to develop China's vast rural and interior regions, aiming to unleash domestic consumption among the wider population. Industrial structures are shifting inland with dozens of new cities emerging and coastal areas developing into sophisticated urban clusters.

Seizing Opportunities

While the rise of China is easy to acknowledge, businesses constantly need to catch up with the speed and depth of change and development in China's large and complex market space.

Whether selling, trading, investing or franchising, China offers opportunities in abundance to Western companies, large or small.

Chapter 2: Researching the Market where to Begin

Doing business with China can seem rather daunting for those new to the market, but taking a strategic approach is the key to making the process manageable.

Companies should conduct reliable research before venturing into business in China. Good research saves costs and improves the efficiency and impact from the start of a project.

Desk Research

General introductory business information concerning China is increasingly available and companies can obtain a reasonable amount of preliminary information through desk research.

Economic research and sector analysis can often be obtained from a large number of leading consultancies, research agencies and public sector trade promotion organisations. The increasing use of e-commerce and B2B websites in China has made identification of (and access to) potential business partners possible across the globe.

A good place to start is the China-Britain Business Council website www.cbbc.org

Another source of information is the Hong Kong

Trade Development Council www.hktdc.com which can assist UK companies wishing to do business with China via Hong Kong.

If you are thinking of doing business with China and you don't know where to start.
Below are frequently ask questions by companies and advisers. Ask yourself and see if you know the answers before you start venturing into China

- What are the unique selling points to your business proposition? Will there be a market for your product and services?
- Are there any legal barriers to your business model?
- Where in China would you start?
- Do you have sufficient resources (management time, project finance and expenses) to fund your China projects?
- Who will be leading the project within your company?
- Do you need to work with a partner in China to succeed? Can you communicate with them effectively?
- Have you evaluated business risks (such as protecting your IP) and conducted research and due diligence?
- Do you know how to secure payment and get the right quality products?
- Rarely will one have answers to all the questions above, and this "knowledge gap" forms the basis of further research and investigation.

However, up-to-date and reliable business information to help guide business strategies and decisions can be hard to find in China, especially given the pace and scale of the market's development. Obtaining dependable information and insights from secondary and publicly available sources can often be more difficult than in Western markets. To gather intelligence, there is greater reliance on primary qualitative research (such as using in-depth interviews).

Consultation and Bespoke Research

Research based on secondary information is often inadequate. Many websites and online materials are written in Chinese; the quality and reliability of content varies greatly and sometimes certain information is simply unavailable. It is therefore essential to verify the initial research findings and conduct further investigation.

Often this requires mapping out a bespoke research brief with the help of specialists, and exploring what additional information you might need to make an effective entry into the market, and how you can make the contacts vital to success.

UK Trade & Investment and the China-Britain Business Council work closely together to offer a range of support services to British businesses in the Chinese market.

Speaking to an Expert

UK Trade & Investment provides support for UK companies through a network of international trade teams (ITTs) based in the English regions. UK Trade & Investment services are also available to companies in Scotland, Wales and Northern Ireland.

In addition to the international trade teams across the country, CBBC has a number of China Business Advisers (CBAs) who have extensive knowledge and practical experience of doing business in China. To arrange a consultation with one of the China Business Advisers, please visit www.cbbc.org

The Overseas Market Introduction Service (OMIS) is a UKTI service delivered by CBBC in China. This service can assist you by undertaking tailored research using extensive network of dedicated researchers across China.

This can be used in a wide variety of ways to help your business with its particular needs when entering the Chinese market. Possible ways in which OMIS can help your business include:

- Market research & analysis - Sector reports - Market initiatives - Regulatory environment - Market opportunities
- Identification of local contacts - Agents - Distributors - Suppliers - Potential partners
- In-market activities - Meeting arrangements - Event organisation, such as workshops, seminars, promotional activities and product launches

Events and Seminars

UKTI and CBBC organise a large number of business events, seminars and workshops in the UK and in China, covering a wide range of business interests and issues. Not only do these events inform companies of business opportunities and the latest information about the Chinese market, they also provide a valuable platform for networking and sharing experience with like-minded peers, not to mention regular access to visiting Chinese delegations.

Market Visits and Trade Missions

Visiting China is an invaluable part of the process of market entry. You will experience the marketplace first-hand, and make the contacts necessary to do business. This is essential, but will be much more effective with careful planning.

UKTI and CBBC do organise regular trade missions to China, where you can benefit from group activities in addition to your own programme.

The UKTI OMIS service can be used to support visits providing bespoke meeting arrangements with appropriate potential partners, agents and distributors or with relevant government officials.

In China, UK Trade & Investment (UKTI) works in partnership with the China-Britain Business Council (CBBC) to deliver trade services. A partner network available through the British Embassy in Beijing, the British Consulate-Generals in Hong Kong, Shanghai,

Chongqing and Guangzhou and through CBBC's presence in 11 cities, this can assist UK companies by providing advice and information on primary and regional cities. Market information and sector.

They also provide the following Trade Development Services to help you develop your ambitions in China.

- Overseas Market Introduction Service (OMIS): a chargeable UKTI-led tailored service to access market and industry information, identify potential contacts or assist in planning an event.
- Passport to Export: a UKTI- led service that provides new and inexperienced exporters with the training, planning and ongoing support they need to succeed overseas.
- Gateway to Global Growth – Where Next? a free service to experienced exporters which offers a strategic review, planning and support to help grow your company's business overseas.
- Events and seminars: including sector-based activities addressed in events and seminars across China and the UK.
- Missions: missions to China help UK companies visit the market, while visits from China allow UK companies to meet with potential partners or potential investors in the UK.
- Business opportunities: They Share opportunities arising from China with UK companies.
- Fiscal Stimulus Initiative: UKTI can help UK

companies of all sizes to identify the opportunities created by fiscal stimulus packages and major spending programmes around the world.

Further useful links:

- British Diplomatic Posts in China: www.ukinchina.fco.gov.uk
- British Chamber of Commerce in China: www.britcham.org
- Export Communications Review: assessment of your company's export communications followed by practical recommendations for improvement (managed by British Chambers of Commerce).
- Export Marketing Research Scheme: provides companies with the facility to collect systematic and objective market research to assist in the development of a market entry strategy (managed by British Chambers of Commerce).
  www.britishchambers.org.uk/exportzone
- Practical support: translation, interpretation and logistics advice are all available from CBBC.
- FCO Country Updates: Reports by UK embassies in key emerging markets, providing authoritative analysis and drawing on high level government and other contacts, providing timely assessment of key issues relevant to UK business.
- The Sustainable Cities Initiative: UK Trade &

Investment's Sustainable Cities Initiative currently encompasses the three Chinese cities of Wuhan, Chongqing and Changsha. The aim of the Initiative, which is underpinned by Memoranda of Understanding is to develop commercial opportunities for UK and Chinese companies to cooperate in the fields of sustainable urban planning and design, green buildings, and environmental technologies, and including urban new build and regeneration, land reclamation, renewable energies, urban transport, water and wastewater management and treatment, and leading the transition to low carbon.

Chapter 3: There are Significant Divides in China's Regional Economies.

Coastal provinces in the Chinese eastern seaboard are the most economically advanced, benefiting from historical trade links and better infrastructure. These regions were among the first to respond to the reform and opening-up policy and have enjoyed sustained growth spurred by export and investment. It is also noticeable that the majority (70 per cent) of the Chinese population live in the eastern part of China. By contrast the vast inland regions in China are more domestically oriented and more abundant in natural resources. However, many of these regions are still developing to catch up with the coastal areas.

There are a number of regional economic hubs within China, where several cities interact to create a wider economic area. The most significant are the Bohai Rim region, the Yangtze River Delta region and the Pearl River Delta region.

The question of "where to start" is often asked by companies who are new to the market, and those who seek business expansion. China offers a wide variety of potential locations, and beyond the more familiar established regions and cities it can be difficult for firms to choose.

Opportunities for UK companies in China's regional cities

Traditionally, business interest from British companies has generally focused on a few business "hot spots", first-tier cities such as Beijing, Shanghai, Guangzhou and Shenzhen.

However, these established markets are maturing; competition from both international and Chinese players is intensifying; and factor input costs, especially the costs of land and labour, are rising.

In addition, the Chinese economy is increasingly seeking growth driven by domestic dynamism, particularly consumption and development in inland and rural areas. Often the rate of development in the lower-tier cities is faster, and international competition is often lower.

On behalf of UKTI, a comprehensive research report was published in September 2008 by CBBC and the University of Leeds. The study found significant opportunities for UK businesses in many cities outside of the traditional international business centres.

Over 270 cities with a population of over one million were examined and the report identifies 35 as most attractive for UK business. Combined, these 35 regional cities account for around 16 per cent of China's population and market entry.

Chapter 4: Choose the Right Location

23%-36% of China's gross domestic product (GDP) are from the regional cities are located on the east coast, particularly in the economically advanced regions of the Bohai Rim, the Yangtze River Delta and the Pearl River Delta, and a number of interconnected "city clusters" are developing.

The remaining cities are more widely distributed through the country. Each one of the 35 featured cities offers UK companies particular opportunities, as well as challenges, in a wide range of sectors. They do, however, share certain key characteristics, including rapid economic growth, lower input costs, large and developing consumer and industrial markets, and strong local government support and policy momentum for regional economic development.

The relative attractiveness of a number of these regional cities has been calculated for four different types of generic business activity likely to be conducted by UK companies in China, namely: local sales of imported products, domestic-oriented production, export-oriented production and research and development. See table on next page.

City Attractiveness by Business Activity

Business Activity	City Profile	Cities Highlighted
Local Sales	• Higher-than-average disposable income • Strong retail sales • Good retail infrastructure • Lower-cost access to seaports	• Dalian • Dongguan • Hangzhou • Qingdao • Suzhou • Tianjin
Local Production for Domestic Markets	• Good logistics network • Low labour costs • Good labour availability • Comparatively low energy costs • Preferential government policies	• Changchun • Shenyang • Tangshan • Weifang • Weihai • Wuxi • Xi'an
Local Production for Export Markets	• Easy access to seaports • Strong concentration of multinational manufacturers • Large pool of educated workers • Good manufacturing infrastructure and facilities • Reliable energy and transportation infrastructure	• Dalian • Hangzhou • Ningbo • Qingdao • Suzhou • Tianjin • Weifang

Research and Development (R&D)	• Large pool of university-educated workers • Reputable universities and science and technology facilities • High government spending on science and education • Concentration of high-technology development zones	• Chengdu • Dalian • Hangzhou • Harbin • Suzhou • Tianjin • Wuhan • Xi'an

Chapter 5: Wider Opportunities in Greater China

Greater China is a term often used to refer to the collective regions of mainland China, Hong Kong, Macao and Taiwan, as these regions share close business, ethnic, political and cultural connections.

Business opportunities in these regions should not be overlooked, and while companies should really treat these markets as separate, Hong Kong, Macao and Taiwan may also provide a gateway to business success in mainland China, as well as in the wider Asia-Pacific region.

Hong Kong and Macao

UK companies find Hong Kong a traditional gateway to business in mainland China. There are significant historical and cultural links between Hong Kong and Britain, and it remains the UK's second-largest market in Asia.

As one of the world's most free economies, Hong Kong offers a great business environment. It benefits from a transparent legal system, English is spoken as an official language and it is a global centre for trade, services, finance and innovation.

Since the 1997 handover, Hong Kong has remained a prosperous business destination and there are ever-closer ties with the economic development of the mainland. A quarter of China's trade passes through Hong Kong, which is also the largest investor in every province in China. Hong Kong companies were the first to move their manufacturing operations to the Pearl River Delta region of China, and there are over 70,000 Hong Kong companies in Guangdong Province alone, employing 11 million people.

There is also a trade agreement between China and Hong Kong – the Closer Economic Partnership Agreement (CEPA) – which gives Hong Kong preferential access to China's markets.

Similarly to Hong Kong, Macao is also administrated under the "one country, two systems" rule and the city-region offers opportunities in sectors such as gaming/leisure, tourism and infrastructure.

Taiwan

Taiwan rose to global economic recognition in the 1980s as one of the "Asian Tigers". Having a stable legal system and financial industry, Taiwan has specific strength in offering competitive and innovative manufacturing solutions to global companies. With a high degree of global supply chain integration, UK companies may find Taiwan an attractive destination to provide value-added products and services.

There is potential to leverage the considerable common ground on business, culture and language that the Taiwanese share with the mainland and other Asian countries.

Taiwan is a major investor in China with more than 70,000 Taiwanese companies operating on the mainland. Up to 70 per cent of Chinese electronics are produced by Taiwanese-invested firms and some 500,000 Taiwanese live in Shanghai alone. Cross-straits relations have improved significantly since 2008, direct flights are now permitted and Chinese investment is allowed to enter the Taiwan market.

Chapter 6: Establishing a Presence

Given China's sheer size, complex and changing business environment, as well as culture and language barriers, it is not an easy market to enter and exit with a quick win. To succeed in China requires careful business planning and execution. Foreign companies need to take time to build up their business network and credentials and to demonstrate their commitment. Often this requires some sort of presence in the marketplace, whether directly through your own business operation, or indirectly, working through a strategic partnership such as an agent or distributor.

Agents and Distributors

An agent is a company's direct representative in a market and is paid commission, while a distributor sells products on to customers after buying them from the manufacturer – their income comes from the profits they make on the difference.

Market entry through working with an agent or distributor can have several advantages, such as reducing time and costs to market entry as well as gaining the local knowledge and network of the agent. However, there are some drawbacks to this approach. Employing a third party results in an additional cost to your products and you may also lose some control and visibility over sales/marketing. It also has implications for intellectual property rights protection, increasing the risk of your product being copied or counterfeited.

Given the above considerations, companies need to select agents and distributors carefully. Some of the frequently asked questions are in the following checklist. You should also conduct due diligence to verify this information.

Background

- Company size, history and ownership (private or state owned).
- Quality and quantity of the sales force.
- Customer feedback and trade/bank references.

Distribution channels

- Regional coverage.
- Types of outlets covered and frequency of calling.
- Transportation and warehousing facilities.

Are they right for you?

- Does the agent/distributor have a genuine interest in representing your product?
- Can they benefit from actively promoting your interests (is it a win-win)?
- Do they also represent any competing companies/products?
- Can you communicate effectively with your counterpart?

Once a working relationship is established, the

28

agent/distributor needs to be managed actively; this may be achieved by the following:

- Visiting as regularly as is practicable at a senior management level – this shows interest in, and commitment to, the agent and the market. This will also provide you with an opportunity to learn about conditions in the market and see how your products are faring.
- Working closely with the agent to show them how they can profit from your products.
- Helping to prepare marketing and sales plans for the agent.
- Providing regular training for the sales staff and after-sales training for the technical staff in the UK.
- Linking performance to incentives and agreeing milestone targets.

Establishing a Permanent Presence

Although it is possible to be represented through agents or distributors, many foreign companies progress to the establishment of a permanent presence in China, as their experience and confidence grow. Having a permanent presence in-market can provide several possible benefits, including:

- Market presence – showing commitment.
- Cutting out the "middle man" – direct access to the end customer/supplier.
- Direct control over corporate strategy and activities.

- Enables trading in local currency and eases the conduct of business transactions.
- Fulfils a legal requirement to have a permanent presence (relevant in certain business activities and sectors).

There are a number of structures that allow foreign invested enterprises (FIEs) to conduct various business activities. These include representative offices, joint ventures, wholly foreign-owned enterprises, and foreign invested commercial enterprises. Each of these structures has unique advantages, restrictions and drawbacks, and it is essential to choose the option best suited to your business aims.

The rules and regulations regarding foreign direct investment and FIEs have evolved gradually since China began opening up to foreign business activities. Since China's accession to the WTO there have been a number of amendments to regulations, easing market entry for international companies across a range of sectors.

Companies that desire a permanent presence have to set up operations as an appropriate legal entity, depending on the intended business scope, and be compliant with Chinese legal and tax requirements. It is usually more difficult to alter a business structure once a legal entity is incorporated or established, so it is vitally important to seek professional advice on your investment structure during the early stages of planning. You must fully understand your intended business activities in China (for the short and long term), whether they are practicable, any legal and sector barriers to entry, and in turn what the suitable vehicle is for you.

UK Trade & Investment and the China-Britain Business Council can offer dedicated one-to-one consulting and incorporation services to assist UK companies establishing various kinds of permanent presence in China.

Representative offices are often the first step taken by foreign companies when establishing a permanent presence in China. They provide a vehicle through which the foreign investor can undertake activities such as market research, customer liaison and support. Representative offices can also organise business visits from company headquarters, which can make the obtaining of business visas for visitors much easier. Public relations work and local administration are also permitted.

However, a representative office cannot conduct sales activities. This means they cannot sign contracts; receive income, or issue invoices and business tax receipts.

Joint Ventures

A joint venture (JV) is an organisation jointly owned by one or several Chinese and foreign partners. A JV can be formed by way of equity contribution, where ownership, risk and profit are shared based on each party's monetary contribution. Alternatively, a JV can also be incorporated with liabilities and profit

31

distribution being decided by contractual agreement.

Joint ventures may be beneficial in a number of ways. A good local partner may contribute market knowledge and strong marketing and distribution channels, and they may help reduce the costs and risk of market entry. In certain restricted sectors, such as automotive and insurance, forming a JV with a Chinese company is still the only permitted route for establishing a permanent presence in China.

Under current regulations foreign companies are unable to employ Chinese staff legally unless the company is registered in China. CBBC's launch pad Scheme enables UK companies to establish a presence in China by having a local CBBC project manager based in one of CBBC's offices and working exclusively on their behalf.

The scheme is a fast and cost-effective way of enabling companies to try out the China market before committing to a permanent presence.

The challenge of establishing and running a successful joint venture is finding and nurturing the right partnership. Partners have to overcome issues such as mismatched expectations and differences in business culture and practices.

The ability to maintain effective communication, and control where necessary, is also crucial. It is essential that you carry out corporate and financial due diligence before you sign up to any partnership. Companies should also plan an exit strategy. Like a marriage, it is better to have a pre-nuptial agreement than a messy divorce.

Foreign Invested Partnerships (FIP)

On 1st March 2010, rules came into effect allowing foreign individuals or organisations to participate in partnership enterprises, offering a further alternative to representative offices, joint ventures, WOFEs or FICEs.

FIPs allow for partnerships between two or more foreign parties (with all organisations or individuals being from outside China), or a combination of foreign and Chinese organisations or individuals. FIPs also allow for foreign partners to join an existing partnership set up wholly by Chinese partners (including the transfer of a partnership stake to a foreign entrant). Investment capital can be in foreign currency or in RMB. It is essential that the liabilities of all partners are carefully addressed before entering into the partnership.

FIPs do not need to be registered through the Ministry of Commerce; they only require registration through the Administration for Industry and Commerce. However, businesses in certain sectors will need to comply with other specific regulations when applying for registration. FIPs are bound by China's industrial policies regarding foreign investment, and are only permitted if the Catalogue for the Guidance of Foreign Invested Industries allows 100 percent foreign ownership. In some restricted sectors JVs are the mandatory vehicle for

33

investment, and FIPs will not be allowed.

Wholly Foreign-Owned Enterprises (WFOE)

A wholly foreign-owned enterprise (WFOE) is a company incorporated in China that is 100% owned by a foreign organisation(s).

Where permitted, WFOEs are now a popular option for foreign businesses, as it gives the investor complete control over their business entity as well as enjoying the full profit from its operation. Generally, WFOEs also give greater protection to the investor's intellectual property rights, compared to a joint venture.

WFOEs are the appropriate structure for companies whose main activities in China are to manufacture and sell products, or provide services such as R&D or business consultancy.

A WFOE allows the foreign investor to issue invoices and receive revenues in RMB (the Chinese currency) that can then be converted and repatriated out of China.

Foreign-Invested Commercial Enterprises (FICE)

Since 2004, foreign-invested enterprises have been allowed to engage in business activities such as wholesale, retail, logistic services, agency services, franchising and direct importing and exporting. To achieve this, new and existing investors can apply to incorporate a business entity under a special category of foreign-owned enterprise, known as a "foreign invested commercial enterprise" (FICE).

Incorporating in China

In the UK, incorporating a company takes a few days, whereas establishing a permanent presence in China, whether a WFOE, a FICE or even a representative office, may take a few months and involves a complex process through which the foreign investor will obtain the various required approvals. It is likely that the foreign company will require professional support on various aspects of business incorporation, including tax planning, legal advice and project management. In some regions in China, foreign companies are required to use a government certified "Filing Agent" to handle the application process.

CBBC provides detailed guidance on various issues regarding business incorporation in China and offers a managed incorporation service. There are also many professional services firms in the private sector that can help with this process.

Chapter 7: Find Customer or Partner

Once you have identified where you would like to start and the best market entry option for your company, the next step is to find potential customers or partners for your company.

The following are all effective ways of finding potential customers, agents, distributors or partners:

UK Trade & Investment's Overseas Market Introduction Service (OMIS):

This can be used to tailor-make a list of potential customers, agents, distributors or partners and arrange a programme of meetings with them for when you visit China. In China, CBBC provides OMIS services on behalf of UK Trade & Investment.

OMIS can also be used to engage CBBC to arrange a technical seminar or product introduction event in China, which can be an effective way of getting your message across to a number of potential customers.

Attend trade shows and exhibitions

Numerous trade shows and exhibitions take place in mainland China and Hong Kong throughout the year and these can be an excellent way to meet potential customers face to face. However, arranging appointments in advance to meet pre-identified contacts at niche industry events is essential if you want to make effective use of your time.

Take part in a UK Trade & Investment-supported trade mission:

UK Trade & Investment supports a large number of trade missions to mainland China and Hong Kong organised by CBBC, trade associations and local chambers of commerce.

The vast majority of problems that foreign companies encounter when engaging in business transactions in China could have been avoided by carrying out some due diligence at the start of proceedings.

There are different levels of due diligence that are appropriate for different situations. If your sole interest is in exporting, the best proof of a Chinese company's ability to pay is whether it is able to raise a letter of credit from the bank. If so, you do not need to check the company's financial standing as the bank will have already done so. At the end of 2008 China's credit database contained the personal records of 640 million individuals and 14.47 million companies and is the largest credit information pool in the world. The database includes loan, credit card use, insurance and bill payment information of individuals and companies and is used by financial institutions in China to make personal credit checks on loan applicants and carry out due diligence on registered Chinese companies.

One simple piece of due diligence you can conduct is

to get a copy of a company's business licence which
will tell you the following:

- The legal representative of the company.
- The name and address of the company.
- The amount of registered capital which is also
  its limited liability.
- The type of company.
- The business scope.
- The date it was established and the period of
  its business licence.

Chapter 8: Due Diligence

You should check that the information contained in the business licence matches what you already know and if it doesn't then find out why.

If you want to verify the information externally you can do so through the State Administration of Industry and Commerce (SAIC). The local AIC bureau is the Chinese equivalent of the UK's "Companies House". All companies in China are legally required to register with their AIC bureau at the municipal level to obtain their business licence.

You will have more security if you know who the legally responsible person is, so find out who you are dealing with. If problems occur, it will be much easier to address issues with the legally responsible person, rather than a middle man, who may go missing when problems arise.

The shareholders of the company are responsible for that amount of liability listed as registered capital on the company's business licence. You can check whether or not the registered capital has been paid up by using a firm of accountants to get a Capital Verification Report.

If you want to establish a business relationship that goes beyond exporting, you will need to carry out further research. A thorough evaluation of your potential partner may be time-consuming and expensive, but doing so will greatly reduce the risk of serious problems in the future. However, it is not enough to obtain a copy of a company's accounts, as they may not be accurate. Accounts are unlikely to be audited to the standards routinely expected in the UK, and companies may have different sets of accounts for different audiences, so it is advisable to use such data in conjunction with information obtained elsewhere.

There are a number of private consultancies that specialise in carrying out operational, financial, legal and technical due diligence checks on Chinese companies, typically by looking at the actual operation of the business, and building up a more accurate picture by carefully interviewing people who work in and with the company.

A particular obstacle that British companies must overcome is the reluctance of many Chinese business partners to agree to thorough due diligence investigations. Failure to gain a full understanding of a potential partner's credit history and professional background can spell serious trouble and financial loss. It is possible to reduce local concerns over due diligence checks through a patient and polite business approach and by stressing the reciprocal nature of the arrangement, but you should expect this stage of negotiations to be lengthy and at times difficult. Good quality consultancy and assistance is available from experienced firms resident in China.

I would encourage you to do as the Chinese do. Expect to spend a lot of time at meetings and banquets with your potential Chinese partners. You might think this is a slow progress, but the Chinese are using this time to establish whether you will make a suitable and trustworthy partner and whether they want to enter into a long-term business relationship with you. It is wise to do the same.

Chapter 9: Employing Staff

Finding the people you need to run your business in China is not significantly different to recruitment in the UK. There are several recruitment agencies currently operating in China, and most operate under the same standards that you would expect of a firm in the West. They will do the sourcing, pre-interviewing of candidates and charge you a percentage of the placed staff's first year earnings or a one-off fee.

In addition, there are a number of recruitment websites advertising for both jobseekers and employers, which can be highly effective.

Another option is to recruit from the huge Chinese population at UK universities. Visa regulations allow Chinese graduates to undertake training and work experience in the UK, before moving to China to take up positions.

One challenge that companies recruiting in China will face is the increasing competition for experienced managers and high-calibre individuals, and as China's economy continues to grow this will only intensify. Skills levels of employees can be an issue at all levels; in many locations demand for skilled workers outstrips supply. Local education establishments will often assist with collaborative programmes, but this can have significant lead time.

Local and foreign companies are recruiting from the same pool of employees who have the right technical and language skills as well as managerial experience. Candidates with the requisite skills and experience will be in demand and command high salaries. If you are not prepared to offer appropriate remuneration, you will have great difficulty hiring people with these skills. Many employees will leave their current companies for ones that are offering better remuneration packages.

You will need to determine what you are willing to pay at the beginning of the recruitment process. It is important to note that salaries in China have increased over the last few years and will continue to do so. It would be advisable to conduct some market research to get a clear idea of appropriate salary levels for the positions you wish to fill so that you can make an offer that is in line with current market rates.

When you are recruiting in China make sure that you carry out all the normal steps that you would if recruiting in the UK.

Ensure that candidates' technical and linguistic capabilities match their claims.
- o It is essential to hire staff with the right language skills. Common mistakes include hiring Chinese staff from outside mainland China who do not speak Mandarin to the level required, or alternatively hiring staff whose business English is not sufficiently fluent for their role.

Ensure that you hire staff at the right level for the role.

- o A recent MBA graduate returning from overseas may not have the experience to navigate the complexities of setting up a company in China without seeking professional advice, and they may not have the capabilities to develop business at a senior level.

Carry out due diligence.

- o To ensure that the staff you are hiring are right for your company, it is essential to ensure thorough due diligence in recruitment, especially for senior managers, including conducting personal background checks and checking all references before offering them the position.

Offer appropriate compensation:

- o Once you have found the right staff you will need to give them good reason to stay with your company. You will need to provide sufficient compensation to ensure that you recruit and retain the best employees. Offering employees the opportunity to train overseas is also very attractive at all levels, although make sure that in return for providing such training they make a commitment to stay with your company. In addition, be sure to invest in the mentoring of Chinese management-level talent; this can be done by giving them experience of working around the organisation and grooming them for global corporate positions. A clearly defined career progression route is also attractive and will help to retain staff.

o A lot of smaller companies setting up an office in China may well just employ one person to deal with all aspects of running the business.

o Although this may be convenient and cost effective, it might not be the best way to run your China operation. Staff selection will prove vital, although the individual may be very willing, honest and capable, they may not be competent or experienced in international business practices. Also, foreign companies in China are at the top of official radar screens. If your employee is not familiar with the relevant Chinese rules and regulations pertaining to the running of an international office or business in China, then you may soon have to deal with issues of noncompliance, which can be very costly. In addition, having one person in control of all financial and legal aspects of the business is obviously risky. An attractive solution to this problem would be to use a service such as CBBC's Launchpad Scheme where companies can have a representative located in one of CBBC's China offices and benefit from the support of CBBC's management and local team.

o If you are employing staff in China you will need to make sure that you comply with China's Labour Law, which came into effect on 1 January 2008. According to this law all employees must have a written contract. If this is not signed within one month, then you will have to pay the employee double their salary for every month they are without a contract. If they are still without a contract after a year then they are automatically deemed to be on an open-ended contract. It is important that the employee receives an original copy of the contract signed by the employer and that the employer gets the employee to sign that they have received the contract.

o It is also very important that, in addition to the contract, all employees are given (and sign to say they have received) a company rulebook detailing all aspects of your company policy and what behaviour is and isn't acceptable. If there are any cases of misconduct you will find it almost impossible to terminate staff employment without written evidence, so make sure that such evidence is documented.

Chapter 10: Language

Communication is crucial to the success of any company, yet business is all too often lost through simple misunderstandings that could have been easily avoided. When working across different time zones, cultures and languages the chances for misunderstanding are multiplied considerably. It is therefore essential to ensure that you have an appropriate communications strategy for China.

In order to communicate effectively in China it is essential to communicate in Chinese. Your translator or interpreter is therefore one of your key assets and should be selected with care, as without them you are effectively deaf and dumb.

The national language of China, Putonghua, is commonly known in the UK as Mandarin Chinese and the characters used to write it are known as Simplified Chinese. This was introduced by the Government in the 1950s and is increasingly used by Chinese communities abroad, although traditional characters are still used in Hong Kong and Taiwan.

If you are working in southern China, in the area between Guangzhou (formerly Canton) and Hong Kong, do not assume that the business language is Cantonese. This region has a vast population of immigrants from non-Cantonese speaking parts of China working at all levels.

For the majority of contacts in southern China,

Mandarin is the language of business. If in doubt, ask first. If you are going to Hong Kong, Cantonese is the preferred Chinese dialect, although Mandarin is increasingly spoken in business circles. English is also commonly used for business and remains an official language in Hong Kong.

In Order To Communicate Effectively In China, It Is Essential To Communicate In Chinese.

While an increasing number of Chinese companies – particularly those with an international outlook – have English speakers on their staff, don't assume that everyone in the company speaks English – especially decision-makers. At the very least, get a Chinese name for your company and prepare a one-page company profile in Chinese for insertion into your company brochure and website. A Chinese translation of your brochure would be even better.

Business cards are essential. It is wise to have your business card translated into Chinese, and to bring plenty with you.

Ensure that all your translation is done professionally. For names it is important to use characters which not only represent the word phonetically but also have a symbolic or auspicious meaning, it is worth talking through the choice for names with your translator. There are numerous translation and interpreting agencies which can carry out suitable translations of personal names as well as general translation work. Many of them will also be able to help you address the branding issues detailed in the next chapter.

Chapter 11: Marketing

The Chinese market is constantly changing, but as income levels rise across China there will be an increasing number of new consumers and first-time buyers who will wish to purchase and experience new products and services. However, the Chinese market is evolving rapidly and to win these new consumers over you will need to continually reassess your marketing strategy.

Tradeshows and exhibitions have already been mentioned in this book as ways of meeting potential customers, but you still need to persuade them to buy your product. You will need to ensure that your sales literature is effective in English and Chinese and decide what kind of advertising is appropriate.

You may need to adapt your product to meet Chinese preferences or requirements in order to be able to sell it. Ignoring local regulations, tastes and cultural preferences is a recipe for failure.

For example, a lot of Chinese consumers attach much more importance to the functional aspect of many products than we do in the UK, so Chinese marketing campaigns may focus on these features rather than on what the product says about you as an individual.

Also, the concept of auspicious and inauspicious symbols is emotionally important to many people in China. Many companies make use of positive symbols and avoid those with negative connotations in order to maximise the success of their products. For example, the number 4 is regarded as unlucky, as the word "four" in Chinese sounds similar to the word for death, but 8 is regarded as lucky, as "eight" sounds similar to the words for prosperity and wealth.

I recommend that you involve a specialist consultancy that can develop a marketing strategy appropriate to your product and to the areas of China where it will be sold.

Cultural Issues Relating to Marketing

The concepts of good and bad luck, or auspicious and inauspicious symbols, are emotionally important to many people in China. Therefore, in order to maximise the success of your products, make use of positive symbols and avoid those with negative connotations.

- 4 is regarded as unlucky, as "four" it sounds similar to the word for death. 7 also has negative connotations.
- 8 is regarded as very lucky, as "eight" sounds similar to the words for prosperity and wealth. 3 is also lucky, as it sounds similar to the word for "life" in Cantonese.
- 9 is also positive as it sounds like the word for "eternity" or "long term", while 6 sounds similar to "good progress."
- Red and yellow/gold are regarded as lucky, but avoid white, which is associated with mourning.
- Use images of auspicious animals: dragon, phoenix, unicorn, tortoise (the Buddhist

symbol of learning), crane and fish.

- Images of the Great Wall indicate stability and reliability.
- Avoid name plaques for opening ceremonies, as these are equivalent to your standing next to your tomb!
- Also avoid black borders around names or photos of people, since this is also associated with death.

Chapter 12: Branding

Conventional marketing wisdom says that global brand consistency is important, but the Chinese language presents some very specific branding issues. In order to create a favourable impression of your company and your brand in China, it is essential to have a name that Chinese consumers can remember.

If a product name can't be remembered, it is unlikely that many people will buy it. It is therefore essential to have a suitable Chinese company and product names in order to sell your products. If your target market is mainland China (as opposed to Hong Kong), it is not advisable to have a Cantonese translation of your company name, as this will not be readily understood outside Hong Kong.

The Chinese translation of Coca-Cola is an example of best practice and highlights the issues involved in creating a suitable name. Coca-Cola in Chinese is "Kekou-Kele" which not only sounds like the English but can also be translated as "Tasty and Joyful", thus creating a name that is easily memorable for Chinese speakers while retaining some degree of global consistency.

Another good example would be B&Q, whose Chinese is name is pronounced "Bai An Ju" and can be approximately translated as "Hundred Peaceful Homes".

A translation of a Western company name that is

perhaps not quite as good as it could be is the translation of Google into "Gu Ge" which, although sounding similar, means "Song of Millet"!

It's advisable to spend some time on getting this right. The name is, after all, the first thing your potential customers will see. There is no right or wrong when translating into Chinese: the name you will ultimately end up with will be a combination of the translator's recommendations and your own preferences.

Chapter 13: Day-to-Day Communications

Once you have made contact with a Chinese company it is likely that your day-to-day phone and email communications will be in English with one of the company's English-speaking members of staff.

If you do not think the standard of English in the Chinese company is up to scratch, you might wish to ask for parallel Chinese texts and get them translated; this could be a valuable investment. An important part of setting up arrangements in China is to ensure that communication issues are covered in detail.

If you are going to sign anything; as obvious as it sounds, make sure you get it translated first, and by an independent translator. Do not rely on your customers' or suppliers' translation and do not be pressured into signing anything that you do not fully understand.

Most failures occur in relationships because of fractured communications and mutual misunderstandings.

If China is likely to become a significant part of your business, you should consider hiring a Chinese-speaking member of staff. There is a rich pool of talent in the huge number of Chinese students graduating from British universities, who are keen to have internships or short-term employment in the

UK before returning to China. These students can also be recruited through specialist recruitment agencies.

You may also wish to take up the challenge of learning Chinese yourself; even having a basic level of communication will create a positive impression and will have the added benefit of making your trips to China more enjoyable.

However, even if you do attain a reasonable level of fluency (which can take over two years with dedicated study), an interpreter or a Chinese-speaking member of staff is still an essential in business meetings.

A Note on Numbers

Large numbers are particularly tricky and often interpreted wrongly, sometimes leading to a mistake between millions and billions. For example, 10 million translates into Chinese as "1,000 ten thousands"; 100 million has its own character as ""; and 1,000 million or one billion translates as " ". There is plenty of scope for confusion. Get numbers written down in Arabic numerals.

A growing number of younger Chinese managers and government officials speak English to a good standard, particularly in advanced sectors such as ICT. But you will usually need to use an interpreter for formal meetings and negotiations in China to prevent the discussions being hampered by misunderstandings. A good interpreter is the key to successful communication. If they have not understood what you have said, your message will be lost on your audience.

There are two forms of interpreting. Consecutive interpreting means you speak and then your interpreter speaks; this is the usual form for meetings, discussions and negotiations.

Simultaneous interpreting involves the immediate translation of your words as you speak them. This requires special equipment and can be expensive. It is generally used only for large seminars and conferences. Interpreting is a skill requiring professional training. Bear in mind that just because someone is fluent in English and Chinese it does not necessarily mean that they will make a good interpreter.

A Good Interpretation Is The Key To Successful Communication.

If you are giving a speech or presentation, remember that the need to interpret everything will cut your speaking time approximately in half (unless using simultaneous interpreting). It is essential to make sure that the interpreter can cope with any technical or specialist terms in the presentation. It is better to be slightly restricted and speak close to a script than to fail to sell yourself. If you are giving a speech, give the interpreter the text well in advance and forewarn them of any changes.

If you decide to bring an interpreter with you (for example an overseas Chinese from Hong Kong or

Singapore), ensure that they speak clear and comprehensible Mandarin. If you are travelling to an area where there is a regional dialect, it is also essential to check whether your interpreter can also speak and understand this.

To get the best out of your interpreter:

Hiring a well-briefed professional interpreter is the best policy. Though this is likely to be expensive, it will be money well spent.

The Chinese will usually, but not always, provide one interpreter for their side. It is advisable to have your own interpreter available to assist with discussions, when possible. One interpreter working for both sides may become tired and start missing the meaning or detail of what is being said. Chinese partners often spring interpreting on junior staff who have studied English but are neither experienced at interpreting nor pre-briefed on the topic of the meeting. With your own interpreter, you should also have some feedback afterwards on the nuances behind what was said (and just as importantly not said) during the meeting.

Try to involve your interpreter at every stage of your pre-meeting arrangements. The quality of interpretation will improve greatly if you provide adequate briefing on the subject matter. Ensure your interpreter understands what you are aiming to achieve.

Speak clearly and evenly with regular breaks for

interpretation. Don't ramble on for several paragraphs without pause. Your interpreter will find it hard to remember everything you have said, let alone interpret all your points.

Conversely, don't speak in short phrases and unfinished sentences. Your interpreter may find it impossible to translate the meaning if you have left a sentence hanging.

Avoid jargon, unless you know your interpreter is familiar with the terminology.

China has no single number for "million" or "billion" which are translated respectively as "one hundred ten thousand" and "ten hundred million". However, it does have unique numbers for "ten thousand" and "one hundred million" - "wàn" and "yì". Therefore, the chance of mistranslation of large numbers is high, so make sure you clarify numbers by writing them down.

Listen to how your interpreter interprets what you have just said. If you have given a lengthy explanation but the interpreter translates it into only a few Chinese words, it may be that they have not fully understood. Or they may be wary of passing on a message that is too blunt and will not be well received by the audience.

Make sure your message is getting through clearly and in a tone that will not cause resentment. But be prepared in the response for the propensity of the Chinese language to be ambiguous.

Chapter 14: Market Access

Before attempting to enter the Chinese market it is important to identify whether the market is open to you and whether restrictions apply.

Certain sectors, for example military, are subject to UK controls and these can be identified from the "UK Strategic Export Control Lists".

The Chinese Government classifies the market for foreign investment or entry into three categories: encouraged, restricted and prohibited. The ability of a foreign company to operate in China varies in line with these, so in some sectors it is possible to set up a 100 per cent foreign-owned company, but in others entry is possible only through a local partner, and in some it is not possible at all. With some professions, for example legal, it is possible to enter the market, but operation is severely restricted.

It is important to understand your freedom to enter the market. Refer to the official "Catalogue for the Guidance of Foreign Investment Industries", published by the Chinese Ministry of Commerce (MOFCOM),

Chapter 15: Business Issues and Considerations

The Chinese market can be more complex for uninitiated companies than other international markets. The challenges of a huge market with a different business culture and language are compounded by a controlled currency and relative newness of international trading in modern China.

Whether buying, selling or investing, whether dealing in physical products or knowledge, it is important to be aware of the complexities and risks. None are insurmountable, but they do require time and resources.

The risk of IPR abuse is commonly cited by UK companies as one of the main deterrents to doing business in China. In reality the situation is complex and in a recent survey UK companies actively involved in the Chinese market placed IPR ninth in a list of challenges.

From having no IP protection law in the late 1970s, China has progressively enacted legislation to the point where it broadly matches or exceeds our own. However, enforcement has been an issue. China is a large country with a strong regional government system (regional and local authorities may not be as committed to protecting IPR as central government, particularly if a factory producing counterfeit goods is a major employer in an area of high unemployment) and a very young IPR history.

Substantial progress in enforcement has been made in recent years, partly driven by the rise of "home grown" IPR developed and owned by Chinese companies themselves. The number of patents being filed by Chinese organisations is rapidly increasing, and a large number of Chinese companies are using the legal system, successfully, for redress where they have faced infringements.

Chapter 16: Intellectual Property Rights

UK companies are increasingly indicating support on IP issues from local Chinese authorities. However, it is still important to consider the threat of IPR abuse of your products or services. As part of your market entry strategy you will need to establish how you can protect your rights, how much it will cost and what other steps you could take, such as including IPR in due diligence checks and monitoring the market for possible infringements.

Trademarks and logos can be a particular issue. Unlike many other countries, the first person to register a trademark in China is the legal owner, and if you have been pre-empted, then lengthy cancellation and court proceedings will be necessary, with no guarantee of success. It is important to consider this before entering the market; whether you are selling or buying as it has been known for Chinese manufacturers to register the trademarks of foreign customers.

It is wise to take a practical, as well as a legal view, on IP protection. In some cases, for example where existing patents are several years old, patent registration in China is not possible; also, smaller companies may struggle with the costs involved. Practical steps include choosing partners carefully; developing business relationships that are of mutual benefit and hence a deterrent to infringement;

retaining key elements of IP; and working with several partners, rather than "putting all the eggs in one basket".

An experienced independent IPR lawyer is invaluable in helping you to establish the best strategy for your company.

Companies can also obtain free advice and assistance from a joint EU and Chinese government-funded project "EU-China IPR2" via www.ipr2.org, which aims at supporting rights-holders and improving IP enforcement in China.

All overseas products imported into China are checked and certified by the domestic and overseas arm of the General Administration of Quality Supervision, Inspection and Quarantine of the People's Republic of China (AQSIQ). Two agencies of AQSIQ, the Certification and Accreditation Administration of the People's Republic of China (CNCA) and the Standardisation Administration of China (SAC) are responsible for certification and standardisation in China.

Generally, but not exclusively, Chinese standards match ISO, ANSI or BS/EN. When importing into China, Chinese standards take precedence over foreign standards, so it is essential that your products adhere to the applicable Chinese laws, regulations, standards and certification requirements.

Chapter 17: Certification and Standards

Chinese standards are divided into Mandatory Standards and Voluntary Standards. Mandatory Standards are those concerning the protection of human health, personal property and safety and those enforced by laws and administrative regulations. Standards that fall outside the above criteria are known as Voluntary Standards. Certain market sectors, such as medical products and food, require extensive registration (and possibly testing) and certification.

The China Compulsory Certificate (CCC) is a compulsory quality and safety mark that is required for a range of manufactured goods before they can be exported to or sold in China. CCC certification is required for a wide range of products that could impact on human life and health, animals, plants, environmental protection and national security. Goods imported into China that require the CCC mark and do not have it may be held at the border by Chinese Customs and may be subject to other penalties.

Both the CNCA and the SAC have English language websites providing comprehensive information on certification and standardisation: www.cnca.gov.cn/cnca/ and http://www.sac.gov.cn/templet/english/

Chapter 18: Currency Exchange and Transfer of Funds

Many Chinese companies prefer to be invoiced in US dollars, particularly if they are already doing business with the USA, although it is sometimes possible to negotiate contracts in Euros or even sterling. Conversion of the Chinese RMB to foreign exchange is strictly controlled by the "State Administration of Foreign Exchange" (SAFE), a government department, which regulates transfer through the banking system. This affects all financial transactions, from the ability to purchase Chinese RMB before travelling, to contractual payments and dividends. Small transactions, such as the use of ATMs and credit cards, are straightforward, but the controlled currency means that you need to be more careful in setting up contracts and investing in the market.

Company dividends may only be paid annually, following audit of accounts by an approved accountancy firm.

Contracts and Payment

Contracts as operated in the UK are relatively new in China. They are, however, essential for successful business there, for the same reasons as in any other market. They also ensure smooth transactions of payments through the Chinese banking system. If payments do not match the contract they may be delayed, or conversion into foreign exchange may be blocked.

Getting Paid and Financial Issues

It is common for negotiation to continue after a contract is signed in China, so it is wise to build into the final figure some provision for concessions. Substantial additions to the contract need extra care as, if they do not match the original contract, payments may be held up in the banking system.

As elsewhere with large contracts involving stage payments, the final stage, which often depends on "sign off", may be difficult to realise, and this needs consideration when agreeing terms.

When drawing up a contract with a Chinese organisation you should observe the following:

- Make it similar to other international contracts, but be very explicit and avoid legal jargon, which may not be understood.
- Include an arbitration clause, as legal action can be very expensive and difficult to pursue.
- Take care with milestones and related payments; this is especially important with royalties contracts, for which payments can attract particular attention.
- Agree and stipulate who is responsible for taxes.
- Agree and stipulate how agency payments are to be handled.
- Ensure the contract is fully understood and agreed with the Chinese organisation. The

contract should be accurately translated and both versions signed.

- Consider the law applying to the contract. Contracts under foreign law are permitted and may offer easier prosecution in the ruling country if something goes wrong, but this will need enforcement in a Chinese court. Contracts under Hong Kong law, which is based on English law, may be a suitable compromise.

Short-Term Finance

When exporting to China normal commercial rules should be followed, and you should discuss the arrangements for security of payment with the international department of your UK bank, the UK offices of Chinese banks or UK-based banks that have offices in China. If you are a first-time exporter to China, the standard method of receiving payment for your goods is by documentary letter of credit.

The Chinese bank will make payment provided that the requirements of the letter of credit are met. However, be aware that a letter of credit is a form of contract between two banks. A bank will make payment provided that the documents submitted to it are in strict compliance with the conditions of the letter of credit. This is regardless of the purchase contract. To prevent the possibility of a payment being made if the terms of the purchase contract are not met, the seller should check the letter of credit against the terms of the purchase contract, ensure that they match, and build in any necessary safeguards.

Open Account and Bills for Collection are other payment methods commonly used between UK exporters and Chinese importers when a trustworthy relationship between the two parties has been developed. Major exports and those requiring long-term finance will require specialist payment and financing.

Pricing

Margins achievable in Chinese markets are likely to be lower than in Western ones. This situation is changing rapidly, and increasingly Chinese companies are prepared to pay more for demonstrable benefits, and it is occasionally possible to command a premium for a unique product or service.

Insurance

The private sector provides credit insurance for exports of consumer products, raw materials and other similar goods. Speak to your banker or insurance broker for more information or contact the British Insurance Brokers' Association for impartial advice. Private sector insurance has some limitations, particularly for sales of capital goods, major services and construction projects that require longer credit packages or are in riskier markets.

The Export Credits Guarantee Department (ECGD), a separate government department that reports to the Secretary of State for Business, Innovation and Skills provides a range of products for exporters of such goods and services. www.ecgd.gov.uk

Chapter 19: Management, Control and Quality Assurance

With the challenges of distance, language and culture, many UK companies are tempted to take a "hands-off" approach to transactions and operations in China. In fact, these challenges increase the need for proactive engagement. A "hands-off" approach allows problems to develop, often to the point where they become major issues.

There is no simple solution, and successful UK companies use a variety of techniques. These can include extensive travelling by UK personnel, a controlling or liaison presence in China (such as using CBBC Launchpad), or providing extensive training and good management of Chinese staff. It is important not to allow milestones to slip by, whether these are attending a board meeting in a joint venture or arranging a quality audit at a supplier.

Sourcing products from China, especially from a supplier inexperienced in dealing with foreign companies, requires particular attention to detail. Specifications are sometimes not understood and need to be very clearly explained and agreed, and a quality management system needs to be agreed and put in place with the Chinese company. Many consultancies will offer to undertake all or part (e.g. the quality management aspects) of this process on your behalf.

Chapter 20: Overseas Business Risk - China

Below are key security and political risks which UK businesses may face when operating in China.

Political and Economic

Check out the latest political and economic updates on China

The General Secretary of the Communist Party and President of China is Hu Jintao who was appointed to a second five-year term in 2007.

Party policy is set by the twenty-five member Politburo and its Standing Committee of nine.

The rest of the Politburo are also appointed for five-year terms, which are due to expire in autumn 2012, when there will be a transition of power to a new generation of leaders. Front runners to replace Hu Jintao and Premier Wen Jiabao (3rd most senior in the Politburo) are, respectively, existing Politburo Standing Committee members Xi Jinping (Vice-President) and Li Keqiang (Vice-Premier).

The United Kingdom recognises that Tibet is a part of the People's Republic of China, and has called on the Government to enter into talks with representatives of the Dalai Lama in order to find a solution to ethnic tensions there on the basis of meaningful autonomy. Companies planning to do business there may wish to seek advice on any political risks involved.

The People's Republic of China claims Taiwan as a province. The United Kingdom recognises the Government of the People's Republic of China as the Government of China, and acknowledges its claim to Taiwan.

Bribery and Corruption

Bribery is illegal. It is an offence for British nationals or someone who is ordinarily resident in the UK, a body incorporated in the UK or a Scottish partnership, to bribe anywhere in the world.

In addition, a commercial organisation carrying on a business in the UK can be liable for the conduct of a person who is neither a UK national or resident in the UK or a body incorporated or formed in the UK. In this case it does not matter whether the acts or omissions which form part of the offence take place in the UK or elsewhere.

The problem of corruption is deep rooted in China and remains a serious threat to business. Nevertheless, the Chinese authorities take a strict approach to dealing with corrupt practices such as bribery, paying commissions and tax evasion and are increasingly likely to investigate and seek prosecution. The most severe financial crimes carry the death penalty.

In April 2010 China's State-Owned Assets Supervision and Administration Commission (SASAC) published new regulations defining the scope of commercial secrets. This followed criticism of the vague definitions used in the trial in March of four Rio Tinto employees who were convicted of stealing commercial secrets and taking bribes.

Under the regulations, "commercial secrets" are defined as technological information or business information, which is unknown to the public, can bring about economic benefits to the holder, is of practical use and to which the holder has adopted measures to maintain their confidentiality. This includes (but is not confined to) information relating to strategic planning, mergers and acquisitions, joint venture investments, stock market listings, financial information, investment decisions, production methods, client information, sales strategies. The definition is wide enough to encompass anything that could hold economic value to a company.

State-owned enterprises (SOE's) are now required internally to classify commercial secrets as either "core commercial secret" or "standard commercial secret", according to their importance. SOEs will need to set a time limit on these classifications. Some of the preventative measures that these SOEs are required to implement include:-

- Requiring their counter-parties to enter into confidentiality agreements during certain negotiations and consultations involving technology transfer, equity joint venture establishment, due diligence etc; and

- The need to establish procedures to protect the disclosure of information relating to listings and issue of stock.

Depending on the perceived value of the commercial secrets, these could also be regarded as "state secrets" and treated as such according to the PRC's state secrets laws. The Chinese Government has also taken steps to require by law that telecoms and internet providers co-operate with investigations into the electronic transmission of state secrets.

Visit the Business Anti-Corruption portal page providing advice and guidance about corruption in China and some basic effective procedures you can establish to protect your company from them.

Terrorism Threat

The Centre for the Protection of National Infrastructure also provides protective security advice to businesses.

The Olympic Games in Beijing in August 2008 saw a spike in terrorist activity in China, associated with the Islamist extremist separatist East Turkestan Islamic Movement (ETIM). The EITM's aim is to establish an independent and self-governing Uyghur province of East Turkistan (Xinjiang region). The majority of attacks have been confined to Xinjiang province, although the EITM has claimed responsibility for an attack in Shanghai in May 2008. Since the end of the Olympics, there have been no high-profile attacks, and there is no reason to suggest that Western interests are deliberately targeted in their campaign.

Protective Security Advice

Commercial Espionage

Monitoring of business executives and foreign visitors is common, by technical or human means. Much of the surveillance is overt. All hotel rooms and offices may be monitored, and business people should be careful not to discuss sensitive commercial information in situations where they might be monitored.

Housing compounds and lifts are also under continuous overt surveillance, and all landline and mobile phone lines have the potential to be monitored; it is fair to assume that emails and faxes are similarly vulnerable.

Internet Service Providers (ISP) co-operate with the Chinese Government to monitor emails and browsing. It is also possible that your staff, suppliers and contacts may be placed under some pressure to provide information or co-operate in some way. The promise to them of money may also be sufficient to promote acts against you. They may have developed sloppy password control or use the Internet in a way that increases the risk of remote attack. There is a possibility of implants who may be operating not in your interests but in the interests of your competitors or against British interests in general. Be sure that your local employees understand what is expected of them in terms of both computer use and sharing company information, and monitor it carefully.

Business Disputes

There is a small but growing incidence of "non-official detentions" of foreigners. This type of intimidation usually occurs as part of a business dispute, usually between Chinese and foreign joint venture partners. Typically, the Chinese partners send thugs or employees to surround the facility, refusing to allow foreign partners to leave until payment has been made. Threats of violence are common in such cases, and stand-offs can last hours or a couple of days.

The police are often unwilling to intervene and usually will not do so unless the situation turns violent. British Nationals doing business in China should be aware that if they become involved in a business and/or civil dispute, and the case actually goes to court, the Chinese government might prohibit them from leaving China until the matter is resolved. There have been instances of British citizens being prevented from leaving China for months while their civil cases are resolved. Civil cases may sometimes be regarded as criminal cases and the defendant may be placed in custody.

Intellectual Property

IP rights are territorial, that is they only give protection in the countries where they are granted or registered. If you are thinking about trading internationally, then you should consider registering your IP rights in your export markets.

There is currently no agreement in place for UK musicians to obtain royalties for recorded performances of their works played on Chinese radio or TV.

Organised Crime

A number of British companies have been attracted by potentially lucrative business offers in China, which have turned out to be scams. I therefore always recommend you research the market as best you can to understand any differences to the business environment in the UK and conduct some basic due diligence before making any financial commitments (e.g. checking that your Chinese counterpart is a properly registered and licensed business).

It is worth bearing in mind the following when considering doing business with Chinese counterparts unfamiliar to you:

- An offer 'too good to be true' may be, in fact, just that.
- Any request to pay a fee to have a contract notarised is liable to be a scam.
- Verify the data of your business partner, make due diligence checks.
- Increase your vigilance when making deals via e-commerce.
- When making purchases use secure payment instruments. When selling, secure the payment before delivery of the products.

- Contrary to what a customer says, it is not always necessary to visit China to finalise a contract. Be wary of a customer who insists otherwise.

If you have any suspicions about a company you are working with, UK Trade & Investment Beijing can help to check the validity of the company's "Business Licence" (issued in Chinese only) by the Chinese State Administration of Industry and Commerce.

I will provide more details in this book on most of the key risks in this chapter.

Chapter 21: Bribery and Corruption

Anyone doing business in China is likely to encounter or hear of corruption in one form or another. Historically, practices such as facilitation payments, bribes and giving and receiving expensive gifts in order to develop relationships were often regarded as a part of doing business. This is still the case in some areas, although the problems vary according to sector, type of business and region.

However, the general perception is that the situation is improving. My advice to companies encountering corruption is simple, don't get involved. Not only are there issues of business integrity to bear in mind, but it is also, of course, illegal. Invariably corruption is related to lack of professionalism, transparency and control, all of which are damaging to long-term business.

The Chinese Government is keen to crack down on corruption, and penalties can be severe. In addition, under the Anti-Terrorism, Crime and Security Act 2001, UK companies and nationals can now be prosecuted in the UK for acts of bribery or other illegal activity committed wholly overseas.

Chapter 22: Scams: How to Avoid Them

Fraudsters and scammers exist all over the world, and China is no exception. There have been a number of instances of British and other foreign businesses being targeted by fraudulent companies and individuals operating from various locations in China. The most common scams are:

"The contract scam" – Fraudulent companies in China make unsolicited enquiries to foreign companies, making orders in large quantities with very beneficial financial terms. The foreign company is often then invited out to China to sign the "contract". When they arrive, they are asked to pay for expensive "gifts" or meals for "officials", in order to move things forward.

When the foreign representative flies back home the fraudsters vanish without trace. Companies should also be alerted when they are asked to pay for any "administration", notarisation or foreign exchange control charges.

Too Good to be True?

Once you know the basics, it is relatively easy to prevent yourself from becoming a victim of scams. If you receive an apparently very attractive order from China (or indeed, anywhere else), or see a website offering goods at unrealistically low prices, ask yourself: is this too good to be true? If it looks too good to be true it almost always is.

Don't get on the plane, or send money, without carrying out appropriate due diligence checks.

"The visa invitation scam" – A fictitious Chinese company may randomly request letters of invitation for visas from UK organisations, so their delegates can visit the UK factory/site with a view to developing business. In reality these individuals have no interest in your company or your product; they are looking for the opportunity to enter the UK. If you are approached by a Chinese company in this manner, ensure that you carry out basic due diligence checks before issuing a letter of invitation.

"The domain name scam" – A foreign company receives an email from a fictitious "internet database company", claiming a Chinese company has filed a request to register your domain name, and with a fee they can block that request. Once you have parted with the cash, the scammer disappears.

Chapter 23: Relationship Building and Deal Making

In a highly competitive business environment, it is more important than ever for us to understand the business culture of our target markets.

Understanding business culture helps us understand, anticipate and respond to unexpected behaviour. It also enables us to behave in an acceptable way and avoid misunderstandings. As the Chinese saying goes: ru jing sui su – "When you enter a region, follow its customs".

However, knowledge of business culture, especially in a country as vast as China, where sub-cultures and practices differ from place to place and where every Chinese person is an individual shaped by different experiences must be exercised with caution. A little knowledge is dangerous. But do not worry if you find the complexities of Chinese business culture daunting. Just behaving modestly, patiently and politely, while not suspending one's business judgement is certain to provide a good foundation for successful business in China.

In China, getting to know someone face to face is often regarded as the only way of finding out whether a person is trustworthy. In general, the Chinese set great store on building personal relationships before entering into a business partnership, often saying, "Let's first become friends, then do business".

You can expect your first, and possibly your second, visit to China to achieve nothing other than getting to know several possible candidates for business partnerships. This may seem a slow and costly way of getting started, but it is worth remembering that taking time to cultivate personal connections as the Chinese do is an excellent opportunity to get to know the people you will be working with. Introductions via a trusted intermediary can play a valuable role in opening doors, but there are no short cuts to relationship building.

You will undoubtedly encounter delays and frustrations when doing business in China. Keeping your temper (equated in Chinese terms with maintaining "face"), even when things go wrong, can pay disproportionate dividends. If you are not sure what to do in any given situation, it is best to err on the side of patience and politeness. Do not be afraid to ask a Chinese colleague for advice on how to handle matters.

Westerners normally build transactions and, if they are successful, a relationship will ensue. However, the Chinese believe that prospective business partners should build a relationship and, if successful, commercial transactions will follow.

This difference underlies many misunderstandings arising from business negotiations. Virtually all successful transactions in China result from careful cultivation of the Chinese partner by the foreign one, until a relationship of trust evolves.

GUANXI

The objective of developing close relationships is to build what the Chinese call guanxi (pronounced gwan shee), which are essentially social or business connections based on mutual interest and benefit.

In a centralised and bureaucratic state, reliance on personal contacts is often seen as the only way to get things done. And in a place like China where the legal system is still relatively weak, the need to rely on guanxi remains strong.

In business, guanxi must be regarded as a two-way relationship. We are all familiar with the expression "You scratch my back, and I'll scratch yours". But in guanxi, the obligation does not cease with the second scratch, and the other side will have expectations that the relationship will continue. It is not about making fair-weather friends. If you expect guanxi to deliver, relationships must be maintained through regular contact.

Both Chinese and foreign companies will often attribute their business success to having good guanxi. But the obligations of guanxi are very real. In the wrong place, at an inappropriate time, with unsuitable people, the obligations can become a trap which is hard to escape.

Chapter 24: The Role of the State

It is easy to underestimate the role that the State continues to play in Chinese business.

Despite the rapid expansion of the private sector, many large Chinese businesses in strategic sectors remain state-owned and, in addition, apparently private firms also often turn out to have an element of state control. The state factor can have a significant influence on the way a company does business, so you should make yourself aware of the wider political (in both the small and large "p" senses of the word) milieu that your Chinese partner or customer operates in. This knowledge will give you a greater understanding of where the Chinese side is "coming from".

On a related point, government officials such as city mayors and party secretaries, in China often wield far more power than their counterparts in the UK do. Good personal relationships are key to successful business in China, and taking the time to get to know key officials is likely to make doing business much smoother. However, a change of local government officials might affect the incentives or agreements offered by the previous administration. Officials are also occasionally arrested for corruption.

Chapter 25: Making Conversation

Most people should be addressed by a title and their last name. You can address people by professional titles such as "General Manager Wang" or "Director Zhao" or, alternatively, if a person does not have a professional title, use Mr., Madame or Miss, plus the last name.

- Stick to safe subjects such as hobbies, family, your hometown, the Chinese landscape and Chinese culture. The Chinese often ask apparently intrusive questions about your age, income or marital status. These questions are not meant to offend, but if you don't want to answer, remain polite and give an unspecific response.

- Avoid talking politics unless you know the person very well. Chinese people are more nervous having political debates openly. In any case, do not criticise China or Chinese leaders. Do not refer to Hong Kong as if it was still run by another administration or Taiwan or Tibet as a separate entity.

- It is fine to tell jokes in informal situations, but they are best avoided when speaking to a group. Also, be aware that cross-cultural jokes are hard to find, and often the point of a joke will be lost in translation.

- The Chinese do not like to say no. Doing so causes embarrassment and loss of face. If a request cannot be met, you might be told that it is inconvenient or under consideration. Alternatively, you might be told "Yes, but it will be difficult". This might seem like a positive response, but in reality means "No" or "probably not".

- Gestures in conversation can have different meanings in China. Nodding means "I hear what you are saying", not necessarily "I agree with you". Laughing can be from embarrassment rather than because something is funny.

Chapter 26: Entertainment

Work and social life tend to remain separate in the West; whereas much of a Chinese person's social life will be used to further personal and business relationships. In China some three-quarters of business deals are sealed outside of working hours. Tea houses, Karaoke bars and restaurants can all be locations where discussions and deals are made.

Banquets have traditionally been an essential part of doing business in China, although the practice varies depending on where you are and who you are dealing with. Very senior people who have not previously made an appearance may be present at a banquet. They may be key to the approval of the business in hand but be too senior to be involved in the actual negotiations. The banquet is an opportunity to impress them and get a feel for how things are going.

Most Chinese are unenthusiastic about Western food, and prefer Chinese food. Typical official entertainment for a foreign visitor will take the form of a banquet with several courses, often consisting of exotic delicacies not usually eaten in the West – or in China, for that matter!

If you are the host at a Chinese restaurant, at the customary round table, your seat should face the door, with the Chinese guest of honour on your right. Guests are seated further away from the host in descending order of seniority, with the most junior having their back to the door. Thought should be given to placing interpreters between guests who cannot speak each other's languages.

If in doubt about the placement of your guests, a friendly invitation for assistance when they arrive often solves the problem.

It is traditional (but now less common) for the host to serve food to the guest. If you are the host and offer a guest a second helping, do not automatically take no for an answer. They may just be being polite.

It is polite to try a little of each dish if it is offered to you. Otherwise, you can discreetly leave any dishes that do not appeal to you.

Frequent toasts, to good health, Sino-British friendship and so on are standard. Locally produced wines or baijiu (a strong spirit) are the usual drinks for toasts. However, many people in China have a low capacity for alcohol. If you host a meal, plenty of soft drinks should be available.

Never arrive late for a Chinese meal. It is common for people to arrive up to 15 minutes early. They also tend to leave en masse as soon as the last dish has been eaten. Chinese hosts make it quite clear when the meeting is over and you will not be expected to linger.

The Chinese eat earlier than we do. Lunch is served from 11.30am onwards, and dinner from about 6.00pm. Most official banquets run from 6.00pm to 8.00pm.

Table manners are a matter of fitting in. If in doubt, follow your host's example. One gaffe to avoid – do not leave your chopsticks pointing into the bowl, as this resembles an offering of incense to the ancestors or the funerary flags on a recently dug grave. Place them horizontally on the rest provided.

If you are invited to a banquet, it is polite to reciprocate. A good time to have a return banquet is on the eve of your departure or at the conclusion of the business in hand. Many senior officials in southern China are moving away from the typical banquet scenario and are now more likely to be found playing tennis (with a top coach) or golf. Find out what form of entertainment your key contacts prefer, as this can help you decide how best to build your relationship with them.

Chapter 27: Gifts

The Chinese like to give gifts, which are used to express friendship, the successful conclusion of an endeavour or appreciation for a favour done.

Often, the symbolic value of the gift is of more importance than the material value.

It is a good idea to bring along small gifts for your hosts (souvenirs from your region, books, pens, ties, or a memento of your company).

Wrap them in a colour traditionally regarded as lucky, such as gold or red. It is not customary to open presents in front of the giver, unless encouraged to do so.

There are few rules on what gifts not to give, but the Chinese expression for "To give a clock" sounds like the phrase for "To attend to a dying parent", so clocks are not popular gifts. Similarly, cut flowers are associated with funerals.

Gift giving is influenced by hierarchy. The most senior person should receive the most valuable gift. If other gifts are also given, they can be smaller and given to other members of the Chinese team.

Chapter 28: Meetings

When arranging a meeting it is advisable to provide the Chinese company in advance with details of the objectives of the meeting, names and ranks of participants and specific areas of interest. Otherwise, it is likely that the Chinese side will issue a long and general report which is unlikely to provide you with the information you require.

Business meetings start on time and it is good practice to arrive at the location early. Formal introductions are standard and it is usual to be introduced to the most senior person first, followed by the rest of the group in descending order of seniority.

There may be people from several organisations present at the business meeting. If it is not immediately apparent who is the most senior person in the room, it is a good idea to try to discover this by asking about the relative roles of those present in the organisation and then to address remarks to that person.

Another pointer is that the person opposite you at the meeting table will normally be the most senior Chinese person present.

Business cards are essential. At the beginning of meetings where those present have not met before, it is customary to exchange business cards when being introduced. It's advisable to take a good supply.

It is a sign of courtesy to have your card translated into Chinese. Many Chinese do not read English.

Present your card with both hands with the Chinese side face up. Spend a few seconds examining the cards you receive. This shows respect for the card's owner. However, whatever you do, don't write on the card, as this shows disrespect to the owner. When exchanging business cards, greeting your Chinese counterparts with simple phrases such as "Ni Hao" (hello), "Zao Shang Hao" (Good morning) and "Xia Wu Hao" (Good afternoon) can help to break the ice.

Chinese green tea is normally offered at business meetings. This is usually served boiling hot in a porcelain mug with a lid. To avoid the tea leaves, which will sink eventually, blow them out of the way or push them out of the way with the lid. The cup will be refilled periodically, but there is no need to take more than a couple of sips.

Chapter 29: Presentations

Sophisticated PowerPoint and video presentations with multiple illustrations are the norm for many forward-looking Chinese companies, and it is advisable to take the same approach to create a good impression. Dual- language presentations and handouts in Chinese are essential.

Chinese audiences are often more interested in the cost-effectiveness of the product rather than the product itself. Therefore it is vital during the presentation to show how your product can save money.

Chinese audiences also like to see case studies of operational projects using your product, preferably in China or a neighbouring country where conditions are similar. Client lists featuring major players will create good reference points for the Chinese side.

Audience reactions vary. The Chinese applaud themselves when they have spoken, as well as clapping in response to others. But do not be put off if your audience is extremely passive.

Throwing questions to the audience, inviting group discussion and asking for questions may not elicit much reaction, although younger participants are often more willing to ask questions. Often, audiences are happier writing down their questions rather than asking them in front of others.

Chapter 30: Deal Making

Historically, China has witnessed foreign deal making which was not in the interests of the Chinese people. The period in the 19th century where foreign powers forced open the Chinese market and occupied Chinese territory is still referred to as the "Hundred Years of Shame". No wonder then, that China can be suspicious of foreign intent. China's recent re-emergence as an economic power is accompanied by a great sense of national pride, and a desire to be treated on equal terms. At the same time, international issues and how they are reported in the Chinese press can influence the mood of everyday interactions with foreigners in China.

Foreign technology and know-how are highly respected, but the starting point for today's deal making can occasionally carry some historical, political or cultural baggage.

Western business visitors are often deadline-driven and unwilling to slow down to the Chinese pace when discussing business. But in China the pace can be fast and slow simultaneously. Those involved in negotiations know how long they can drag on when the Chinese side is consulting internally or has other reasons for delay. But Chinese negotiators can move with lightning speed on other occasions and exhaust Western business visitors and local partners in consecutive midnight meetings when a deadline is looming. Chinese negotiators use time constraints more strategically than their Western counterparts, who should be aware that speedy conclusion of business can result in extremely tight equipment/service delivery dates.

Another different approach to doing business is that in a buying decision Westerners tend to look for clear alternatives, while Easterners may examine ways to combine both options.

For example, a Chinese panel may feel that a supplier who combines claims of best quality with a low price may either raise the price during the contract or fail to implement the contract.

They will therefore often prefer to choose a supplier whose price is neither the cheapest nor the most expensive. In addition, a Chinese panel may avoid awarding each supplier more than one contract, in order to minimise dependence on a single supplier. Such an approach may make a Westerner think that a Chinese negotiator is being illogical, evasive or devious, when he himself believes he is being quite straightforward.

Chapter 31: Negotiating Techniques

Mobilise Local Assets

The challenge of learning to speak Chinese fluently, the complexities of the Chinese way of doing business, and a strong sense of national pride mean that a foreigner will only extremely rarely be accepted by Chinese interlocutors on equal terms. The solution is to find a reliable Chinese ally to work with you. An effective Chinese colleague will often be able to analyse body language at meetings, work out who in the other negotiating team holds real power (not always the boss), and help smooth out any inadvertent wrinkles.

Face to Face

Face is an essential component of the Chinese national psyche. Having face means having a high status in the eyes of one's peers, and is a mark of personal dignity. The Chinese are acutely sensitive to gaining and maintaining face in all aspects of social and business life.

Face is a prized commodity, which can be given, lost, taken away or earned. Causing someone to lose face could ruin business prospects or even invite recrimination. The easiest way to cause someone to lose face is to insult an individual or criticise them in front of others.

Westerners can unintentionally offend Chinese people by making fun of them in a good-natured way. Another error can be to treat someone as a subordinate when their status in an organisation is high. Just as face can be lost, it can also be given by praising someone for good work before their colleagues.

Giving face earns respect and loyalty. But praise should be used sparingly. Over-use suggests insincerity on the part of the giver.

Conversely, the presence of a Westerner should be exploited to the full. Chinese interlocutors will often see a visit by a foreigner as an indication of sincerity and commitment by the Western company. Perversely, they often do not accord mainland Chinese or Hong Kong representatives the same status as a foreigner.

The ideal sales team, therefore, is often a Chinese to take care of the working level contacts and a foreigner to do honour to the higher echelons.

The Pecking Order

Mao Zedong's thoughts on discipline, published in 1966, provide a valuable insight into structures which persist in Chinese organisations even to this day. "The individual is subordinate to the organisation. The minority is subordinate to the majority. The lower level is subordinate to the higher level." This quotation, which conforms with long-standing traditional social values, indicates why Chinese society and companies are very hierarchically organised, and why Chinese people seem to be more group- oriented than individualistic and often do not like to take responsibility. Similarly, people are seldom willing to give an opinion before their peers as it might cause loss of face with a valued ally.

Tricks of the Trade

Chinese negotiators are shrewd and use a wide variety of bargaining tactics. The following are just a few of the more common stratagems...

Controlling the meeting place and schedule

The Chinese know that foreigners who have travelled all the way to China will be reluctant to journey home empty-handed. Putting pressure on foreigners just before their scheduled return can often bring useful benefits to the Chinese side.

Threatening to do business elsewhere

Foreign negotiators may be pressured into making concessions when the Chinese side threatens to approach rival firms if their demands are not met.

Using Friendship to Extract Concessions

Once both sides have met, the Chinese side may remind the foreigners that true friends would reach an agreement of maximum mutual benefit. Make sure that the benefit is genuinely mutual and not just one-way.

Showing Anger

Despite the Confucian aversion to displays of anger, the Chinese side may put on a display of calculated anger to put pressure on the foreign party, who may be afraid of losing the contract.

Attrition

Chinese negotiators are patient and can stretch out discussions in order to wear their interlocutors down. Excessive hospitality the evening before discussions can be another variation on this theme.

Chapter 32: Counter Play

Here are some useful tactics that may help foreign negotiators dealing with the Chinese:

Be Absolutely Prepared

At least one member of the foreign team must have a thorough knowledge of every aspect of the business deal. Be prepared to give a lengthy and detailed presentation, taking care not to release sensitive technological information before you reach full agreement.

Be Willing to Cut your Losses and Go Home

Let the Chinese side know that failure to agree is an acceptable alternative to making a bad deal.

Cover Every Detail of a Contract Before you Sign It

Talk over the entire contract with the Chinese side. Be sure that your interpretations are consistent and that everyone understands their duties and obligations. Make sure that you get professional legal advice from someone who understands the law (and the language) under which the contract was written.

Be Patient

It is generally believed in China that Westerners are always in a hurry, and the Chinese party may try to get you to sign an agreement before you have had adequate time to review the details.

Chapter 33: Contracts

Chinese and Westerners often approach a deal from opposite ends. To a Westerner, starting with a standard contract, altering it to fit the different circumstances, and signing the revised version, seems straightforward.

Commercial law is ingrained in our thinking. But traditionally, commercial law scarcely existed in China and certainly indicated bad faith. The early appearance of a draft legal contract was seen as inappropriate or, more likely, irrelevant, because it carried no sense of commitment. The business clauses might form a useful agenda. But obligations came from relationships, not pieces of paper.

Nowadays, business contracts are accepted as the norm. But returning home with a signed piece of paper is not the end of the matter. It is not unknown for the Chinese side to view a contract as a snapshot of an agreement that was made at a particular time, and under particular circumstances. Further concessions may then be requested; a difficult prospect for the Westerner who has shaved his margin down to the bone.

Key terms and conditions in an import contract

Chinese importers tend to use standard form contracts in their transactions. Foreign contracts are seldom accepted for fear of being trapped by unfamiliar contract stipulations. Adding special provisions to the contract form is normally acceptable. You can expect to see the following key terms and conditions in a Chinese import contract:

Terms of Price and Shipment

Chinese import businesses often conduct transactions at Free on Board (FOB) prices in consideration for using Chinese shipping companies. Cost and Freight (CFR) and Cost, Insurance and Freight (CIF) terms are accepted only if the freight is proved to be cost-effective.

Insurance

Chinese importers generally have "open insurance" for their import cargoes – i.e. importing companies submit notifications of import cargo shipments and other relevant documents which are then acknowledged by the insurance company as insurance orders, and against which the insurance premium will be settled with the insured.

Terms of Payment

This is normally by letter of credit (L/C).

Inspection

Certificates of quality, quantity or weight issued by manufacturers or public assessors are normally required as part of the process of setting up a letter of credit. However, if the goods are discovered not to be in conformity with the certificates after re-inspection by Chinese inspection authorities, the buyer will either return the goods to the seller or lodge claims against the seller for compensation on losses on the strength of inspection at the port of destination.

In the case of equipment imports, Chinese companies often insert a clause in the contract withholding a portion of the payment; normally 5 to 10 per cent of the total contract value, which will be paid only when the equipment is installed and commissioned. This retention sum tends to become a permanent rebate, so beware of allowing too high a figure.

Dispute resolution

In cases of dispute, the formal contract has a provision that a solution must be sought through friendly consultation. If this does not work, arbitration is then adopted to settle the dispute. Litigation is used only as a last resort.

Chapter 34: Return Visits

Inviting the Chinese side for a return visit to your company in the UK will demonstrate your intent to reciprocate the hospitality of the Chinese side, and will also strengthen the relationship.

UK visas

The UK visa service has been complimented by major Chinese investors such as Huawei for its efficiency. Biometric data (fingerprints and photographs) is now required for all visa applications and this can be done at Visa Application Centres across China. Full details on the visa application process can be found at www.vfs-uk-cn.com

While the majority of visas are granted, some common problems arise which may prevent or delay the granting of visas to the UK. Some Chinese companies may rely on local agents for advice, rather than the Embassy website (www.uk.cn). The quality of these agents varies and they are often more of a hindrance than a help; recommend your visitors use official channels. On top of this, assistants or secretaries may miss or incorrectly enter vital information, so forms should be checked personally by the applicant. If assistants or colleagues are also applying, a cover letter to the visa section explaining that the applications are linked can help. Finally, visitors should allow plenty of time for their application, especially if they require several visas to visit multiple destinations.

Chapter 35: The Concept of Hosting

The Chinese take the concept of being host (and you being in the role of a guest) very seriously.

Companies doing business in China are often treated to a wide range of assistance, including hotels, transport, meals and evening entertainment. Chinese companies can often lean on an extensive network of relationships to provide these without incurring direct costs, or at a substantial discount.

Unfortunately, when they are visiting the UK they expect the same, and most UK companies do not have the budget to handle two weeks of all-in travel for contacts they have never done business with and are not sure they ever will do business with. Therefore, it is best to be cautious about the extent to which hospitality is expected. Don't be rude, but do take the trouble to explain that things are different in the UK.

However, showing you care is not expensive. Making sure your visitors are greeted at the airport and making an effort to see them off when they leave is seen as basic hospitality in China. Organising some sightseeing or shopping for your guests and treating them to a meal in a good Chinese restaurant will also be well received.

A range of UK Government support is available from

a portfolio of initiatives called Solutions for Business (SfB). The "solutions" are available to qualifying businesses, and cover everything from investment and grants through to specialist advice, collaborations and partnerships. UK Trade & Investment is the government department that helps UK-based companies succeed in the global economy, and is responsible for the delivery of the two SfB products "Developing Your International Trade Potential" and "Accessing International Markets".

They also help overseas companies bring their high-quality investment to the UK's dynamic economy; acknowledged as Europe's best place from which to succeed in global business. UK Trade & Investment offers expertise and contacts through its extensive network of specialists in the UK, and in British embassies and other diplomatic offices around the world.

Chapter 36: China-United Kingdom Fact File

China is the second largest economy in the world in nominal US dollar terms. In 2009, China's economy grew by 8.5%, the best performance of all the world's major economies.

China is approximately the same size as the US, with a population of 1.3 billion. There were 122 cities in China with over one million people in 2008.

Bilateral trade in goods and services between the UK and China was US $51.8 billion in 2009. The UK exported £7.7 billion to China in 2009.

The UK ranks alongside Germany as the largest European investor in China (in cumulative terms), with at least 25% of the EU total. The total realised stock of UK investment in China reached US$16.9 billion at the end of Aug 2010.

Chinese investment into the UK was $44 million in 2009, 9.3% of total Chinese investment to EU. By the end of August 2010, Chinese investment into the UK by stock was US$1.13 billion, and 400 Chinese firms are based in the UK.

China is currently the sixth largest investor in the UK by number of projects, with 1,572 jobs associated with Chinese investment.

In the last three years, Chinese companies have committed to over 50 R&D collaboration projects with a further 50 in the pipeline.

China's investment in clean energy in 2009 was $34.6 billion, the highest in the world. China had no motorways before 1988. By 2009, it had 75,000 km, the second largest network in the world. This could increase to 100,000 km by 2020.

By the end of September 2010 there were 89 million cars in China - 13 million of these were sold in the first nine months of 2010. China overtook the US to become the largest car market in 2009. China currently produces over one million cars a month.

China has the largest mobile phone market: over 833 million subscribers (as of September 2010) and the highest internet usage, 420 million users (as July 2010).

China has overtaken the US to become the second largest luxury goods market in the world after Japan.

In 2008/9, there were 85,000 Chinese students in the UK.

Chapter 37: Basic Mandarin

The written language is uniform throughout China; however, as in any other country, Chinese dialects vary from region to region. The standard language, Putonghua (often called Mandarin), is based on the Beijing dialect and is spoken by most people across the country. This is the language of business and if you would like to learn some Chinese, Putonghua is the language to study. There are numerous free-to-access websites designed to help you learn Putonghua, and some simple phrases are below.

English Characters	Pinyin Phonetic
Hello	Ni hao Nee how
How are you?	Ni hao ma? Nee how ma?
Goodbye	Zaijian Sigh jyen
Thank you	Xiexie Share share
You're welcome	Bukeqi Boo ke chee
Sorry	Duibuqi Dway boo chee
No problem (it's okay)	Mei guanxi May gwan shee
I would like to go to…	Wo xiang qu... Wor sheang choo
Hotel	Fandian Fan d-yen
Too expensive	Tai guile Tie gway-la
Toilet	Cesuo Sir swor
Ladies/Gents	Nu/nan Noo/Nan

Chapter 38: Conclusion: China is Here to Stay

With more and more companies from all parts of the world moving to China, the topic of doing business in China is as timely as ever.

New entrants to China keep in mind that China is a mosaic of markets, the importance of business culture and etiquette and taking a market based approach, that procedures in China take time, patience and money, and my favourite, the importance of building a strong local management team. While none of these tips are particularly new, they are worth repeating because they are often forgotten when companies get into day to day operations in the country.

A Mosaic of Markets

Martin Roll, a business and brand strategist who provides advisory to global and Asian brands on China, said that companies have to look at China more like a mosaic of cultures, adding that there is no single consumer profile.

I agree in general with Roll's comment, but believe it dangerous to take that analysis too far. Regional and local differences are quickly being homogenised as more Chinese and foreign companies create national brand strategies. Instead, I prefer to think of China as being divided between a foreign/local market that wants the latest and greatest products from around the world, and can afford them and a purely local market which tolerates lower quality and lower technology products because affordability is the key concern. China's vast income disparity where 400 million of its population has average per capita incomes of £6,000, while another 900 million have average per capita incomes of £600, creates these two markets.

Business Culture and Etiquette

In "China Uncovered: What you need to know to do business in China," Professor Jonathan Story highlights the importance of "face," describing it as a mix of public perception, social role and self-esteem that has the potential to either destroy or help build relationships. That is certainly true. To that comment, I added the importance of developing mutual trust, which begins with having mutual respect for your counterparts in China. For all of its size and economic prowess, China is still a work in progress. As a result, managers coming from more developed economies frequently underestimate their China partners and counterparts. That can be fatal.

Taking a Market Based Approach

It is important for companies to analyse the China market separately, in isolation from their home markets. Even though China is now the second largest economy in the world, it is still embryonic in nature and in a very different stage of development than a country like the United Kingdom for example. A product that sells well and is reasonably priced in the U.K., therefore, may not be suitable for the China market and may be too high priced. Often, products from developed countries have features and quality and technology levels that a large number of Chinese consumers simply cannot afford. If a company wants to address the entire Chinese market, which I urge our clients to do, then thought needs to be given as to how to tailor products to the China market.

Procedures in China Take Time, Patience and Money

China is not a flash in the pan, it will not go away. While there will certainly be ups and downs, there's little question in my mind that China's economic development in the 21st century will mirror that of the U.S. economy in the 20th. Given the fact that China will ultimately be the single largest market for any product, companies need to take a long term approach to building their businesses in the country, and must focus first on building a solid foundation.

Build a Strong Local Team

I cannot overemphasize its importance. Part of building a solid foundation in China is building a strong local management team that is empowered to make decisions by the home office. Once you have it, you'd be surprised how much easier doing business in China becomes.

Good Luck!